RAISE YOUR INNER GAME

Carrie —
Here's to the nomadic life!

All the best —

10/29/17

RAISE YOUR INNER GAME

How to Overcome Stress and Distraction,
Work at Your Highest Level, and
Live a Life You're Proud of Every Day

DAVID LEVIN

MINNEAPOLIS PRESS

Copyright © 2017 by David Levin / Day Eleven, Inc.

All rights reserved. No part of this book may be reproduced or transmitted in any form or by any means, electronic or mechanical, including photocopying, recording, or any information storage and retrieval system, without permission in writing from the publisher.

MINNEAPOLIS
PRESS

Published by Minneapolis Press
510 South Rusk Avenue
Viroqua, WI 54665, USA

www.davidlevin.com

EBOOK AND AUDIO EDITIONS ALSO AVAILABLE

Minneapolis Press supports copyrights because they fuel creativity and innovation. Thank you for buying an authorized edition of this book and for supporting copyright laws by not reproducing, copying, scanning, or distributing any part of it without permission.
You are supporting writers and a vibrant culture.

No patent liability is assumed with respect to the use of the information contained herein. Although every precaution has been taken in the preparation of this book, the publisher and author assume no responsibility for errors or omissions. Nor is any liability assumed for damages resulting from the use of the information contained herein.

Jacket design: Jon Valk
Illustrations: Joni McPherson
Author photo: Richard Bock

ISBN 0-9819892-1-7

FIRST PRINT EDITION
September 2017

Contents

INTRODUCTION
The Power of Raising Your Inner Game 1

PART ONE: The Inner Game and How it Works
1. The Inner Game Framework 17
2. The Levels 23
3. The Elevator 40
4. Inner Game Moments 43
5. Inner Gravity 49
6. Summary, Part One 55

PART TWO: Inner Game Skills and Tools
7. A Picture of the Goal 59
8. "No. Quiet." 61
9. Lifts 67
10. Focused Sitting 73
11. The Inner Game Tracker 83
12. Action Steps 92
13. The Road Ahead 97

CONCLUSION
Raise Your Inner Game! 103

Acknowledgments 107
About the Author 109

The height of a man's success is gauged by his self-mastery.

LEONARDO DA VINCI

INTRODUCTION

THE POWER OF RAISING YOUR INNER GAME

The year was 1992, and my life was in trouble. I'd been working professionally for fifteen years as a touring musician, producer, and singer-songwriter, with enough success at times to have realistic hopes of greater things to come. But those times were clearly past: I was now off the road, waiting tables and playing part time in a wedding band. That might not sound so bad, to be playing in a wedding band—you're still being paid to play music, which is pretty great. But trust me, for someone with rock star dreams, a wedding band is about as low as you can go.

The bigger problem wasn't the gig, though; it was that I had lost my direction. My identity had been tied up in music for essentially my entire life, but now it was slipping away, and I had no idea what to do about it. On top of that, my finances were a mess. I was spending money I didn't have, piling up a troubling amount of debt. Healthwise, I was starting to put on excess weight, which had never happened before. I was also struggling with what had become a pretty serious Coca-Cola habit (drinking several Cokes a day; going to bed at night thinking of the Cokes I'd drink the next day). And I know, in the big scheme of things, these are small-time problems. I wasn't starving. I wasn't living on the street. I hadn't lost everything to addiction. I didn't have a life-threatening illness. In fact, from the outside, I'm sure people would have said that things looked good. My future wife, Margret, and I had been together for several years. We were living in our first house, a cute little two-bedroom in northeast Minneapolis, and were, by all appearances, a happy young couple, cheerfully building our lives together. But for me, internally, it was a different story. I was struggling, and badly. It felt like my life was slipping out of control, and, looking to the future, I couldn't see how things would get anything but worse.

But then I had a strange experience that put my life on a completely different path.

I was walking through our house in the middle of the day when I suddenly had the urge to weigh myself. *I wonder what I weigh right now?* The urge itself wasn't surprising: I'd been on a diet for a few weeks at that point, so my weight was on my mind. But the thing is, I had already weighed myself that morning. And the night before. And the morning before that. I really didn't need to do it again, especially not right then in the middle of the day. Many diet experts will tell you that weighing yourself even once a day is too much, let alone twice a day. Three times is just ridiculous. There was no rational universe in which it made sense for me to weigh myself at that moment. Yet there I was, feeling pulled to do just that—and the pull was strong.

Where is this coming from? I wondered.

And the answer changed everything.

Oh! It's coming from inside of me. *It's like there's another person in there, pulling me to weigh myself.*

That was the moment when I awoke to the reality of how the inner game works. It was like the famous scene in *The Wizard of Oz,* when we suddenly see the man behind the curtain, furiously manipulating the controls, and realize what's been going on all along. It was absolutely clear to me that, in a very real sense, there were two different people inside of me—one who was doing the pulling and another (me) who was feeling the pull—and that somehow this discovery was going to be the key to turning my life around.

Interestingly, I'd heard about this idea before. In his classic 1974 book *The Inner Game of Tennis,* Timothy Gallwey wrote about having essentially the same observation. He was noticing how his players tended to scold themselves when they made mistakes ("What's wrong with you? Why can't you keep it together?"), when he suddenly thought, *Who are they talking to? There are two people in there!* He called the two different selves "Self 1" and "Self 2," and his book went on to sell over a million copies and influence countless athletes and competitors all around the world. Years later, Eckhart Tolle would write of a similar observation in his seminal bestseller, *The Power of Now*. In a moment of intense personal distress, he said to himself, "I cannot live with myself any longer," and suddenly noticed this same two-fold nature: "If I cannot live with myself, *there must be two of me*: the 'I' and the 'self' that 'I' cannot live with." His experience transformed his life and put him on the path to becoming one of the world's best-known authors and teachers on the subjects of spirituality and self-improvement. So the experience wasn't unique to me, and it was an idea I was loosely familiar with already. But reading about something and experiencing it for yourself are two very different things. When I saw this *other* person inside of me, it hit me like a bolt of lightning. And from that point on, things started to change.

With music, I went from feeling lost and playing in a wedding band to having a respectable career. I've released four albums of original music, the last two hitting the Top 10 charts on college radio. I've also received awards as both a songwriter and performer, have worked with world-class musicians, writers, producers, and industry professionals, and have had incredible experiences all along the way. (Fun fact: I once sang the national anthem at a Minnesota Twins game at the old Metrodome Stadium in Minneapolis.) It's not the rock star career I was originally dreaming of, but it's one I'm genuinely proud of, and it's lightyears beyond anything that seemed likely in 1992.

I also became an author and speaker, which was a complete surprise. I'd never written a word before (other than lyrics), nor had I imagined that I ever would. But I've now written two books of my own plus four with my friend and partner, John G. Miller, one of which (*QBQ! The Question Behind the Question*) has sold more than one million copies worldwide, and I've been speaking professionally for over fifteen years.

In my personal life, Margret and I have been together for nearly thirty years now, and happily so, which is not something many people can say. And yes, we were already together back when this all started, but that was no guarantee we'd stay together, especially given my background. First, consider that I spent all of my formative years on the road with a band, which, let's just say, is not the best place to learn long-term relationship skills. On top of that, growing up I had terrible role models for successful relationships. My mother married five times. My father married four times. Even my grandmother married five times. So I had literally no idea how to have a successful relationship. Yet here I am, twenty-nine years later, the first person in three generations of my family to get married once and stay that way. And not only have we stayed happily married, but we've built a truly lovely and fulfilling life for ourselves and our children, which is the best part of all, and the thing I'm most proud of and thankful for.

I don't tell you all this to make myself sound like some sort of special person, because I don't see myself that way at all. I just want to illustrate how much things changed once I saw how the inner game works. It raised the quality of my work, which helped me be more successful and feel better about what I was doing. It helped me be more present and positive with people, so I could collaborate more effectively and do a better job of serving and supporting others. It helped me build stronger relationships and be a better role model (which is especially important to me as a parent). And it completely transformed how I feel about myself and my place in the world. Basically, I stopped feeling like a loser and started to feel proud of myself instead.

This didn't all happen overnight, of course. It took years, and in some aspects decades, for me to fully understand what I'd seen that day and to incorporate the lessons into my life. And it's taken several more years to condense it all into the book you have in your hands. But that Wizard of Oz moment is when it started. And looking back, I can honestly say that everything I'm proud of in my life is a direct result of learning how to raise my inner game.

So, how about you? What would you like to be more proud of in *your* life? Maybe you want to do better and more impressive work, so you can make a bigger difference in the world. Maybe you want to feel better about yourself as a person. Maybe you're more interested in the emotional and social aspects of your life—you want to be happier and more fulfilled, and to have more meaningful relationships. Whatever it is, raising your inner game is the key to getting there, and the purpose of this book is to help you do that.

"... STRONGER THAN OUR WEAKEST MOMENTS..."

One of the hardest things to understand about the human condition is that someone can accomplish so much and still feel like a failure. We think of this happening in the context of the rich and famous, but it's every bit as relevant (and baffling) for you and me. It begins to make sense, though, when you recognize the critical role the inner game plays in self-esteem.

For most people, self-image is based not on what we accomplish, or even on the kind of person we appear to be, but on how strong we are, mentally and emotionally. We can be successful by every other standard and make a real difference in people's lives, but if we're weak with our inner game, giving in to our lower impulses, *that's* what we identify with—and we're ashamed of ourselves for it. "We are stronger than our weakest moments, better than our darkest days" is a line from one of my songs ("The Best in Us"), and it resonates because of our deep, unconscious belief that the opposite is true. Now, it's clearly nonsense to measure our entire self-worth by our weakest moments. But, right or wrong, this *is* often how we feel, and it adds a heavy weight to our lives.

A moment ago, I asked what you'd like to be more proud of in your life. I'm guessing that *yourself* was high on the list. This, for me, may be the biggest benefit of raising your inner game: As you do the work and get stronger at resisting those lower impulses, the shame naturally starts to lift, and you feel proud of yourself in a way you never have before—not for what you've done but for who you truly are as a person.

"READ IN AN HOUR, USE FOR A LIFETIME"

Raise Your Inner Game is not your typical self-improvement book. For one thing, it's quite short and to the point (once you get beyond this introduction), and the reason for that has to do with the lessons I learned from working on *QBQ!*

I mentioned that I've written four books with my friend John G. Miller. *QBQ!* was our second book, and it's a similar size to this one. But our first book together, *Personal Accountability*, was much longer—and much less successful.

When we started that project, we wanted the book to be "Impressive!" which to us at the time meant "long and serious-looking," so we filled it with everything we could possibly say on the subject. When we were finished, the book was big and handsome, but the response was disappointing—it sold a few thousand copies and essentially fell flat. Two years later, though, John had the idea to re-write it in a shorter format. So we combed through the original manuscript, picked out the parts we felt were essential to the message and removed everything else. That new, shorter book—with the same core material—went on, as I mentioned, to sell more than a million copies and have a significant impact for companies and individuals all around the world.

That was a powerful lesson for me, and it's been my guiding principle in developing this book. Rather than filling it out with stories, opinions, and everything else I could think of to say, I've included only what you truly need to raise your inner game, both now, as you get started, and in the months and years to come.

The second thing that's different about *Raise Your Inner Game* is the exercises. There are a handful of short exercises and reflection questions in Part One that are designed to significantly increase the impact of what you're reading. Information itself is helpful, of course, but it tends to stay in your head where its impact is limited. The most powerful changes come when you move the ideas out of your head and into your living reality, and that only happens through experience. So, in your reading, as you come across the exercises and reflection questions, please do them right then if you can, and if not, as soon as possible. Remember, at the time of my Wizard of Oz moment, I was already familiar with the underlying idea of what I was seeing, and had been for years. But *experiencing it for myself* is what made things start to actually change for me. The exercises and questions in this book are here to help you create a similar change in your life.

Finally, the book is strongly oriented toward action. It's not an exploration of ideas or an academic examination of the topic. You won't find chapters on things like the cultural trends in personal development or the origins of peak-performance training. (Just reading that sentence puts me to sleep.) Instead, it's a focused, step-by-step process, designed to get you *doing things differently,* so that you can be happier and more successful—starting today.

THE EVOLUTION OF THIS BOOK

In the beginning, I knew what I wanted the book to be—it was essentially everything I'd learned, adapted, and developed for myself over the years, translated into a simple, *QBQ!*-like framework. (Really, it's the book I wish I'd had those twenty-some years ago.) But I didn't feel that I had enough experience with the material to write the book right away. Maybe the framework wasn't clear enough. Maybe the ideas worked for me but wouldn't help others. Maybe people wouldn't be interested in the first place. So my first step was to run a test in the form of a coaching program, working with a small group of individuals over an eight-week period.

The 1.0 version of anything is never perfect, of course, but the test proved to me that people were, in fact, interested, that the framework made sense, and that the material was helpful. My favorite example was a woman named Bridget. I was initially concerned about Bridget because she was already so well-versed in other self-improvement programs that I was afraid she wouldn't find anything new and helpful in mine. But after the course ended, she went on to lose 58 pounds (though we'd never talked about weight loss), plus she enrolled in and ultimately completed a Ph.D. program—and she credited both accomplishments to what she'd learned in the course.

Needless to say, I was thrilled for her, and gratified that the material could make that kind of difference. But to be honest, I wasn't completely surprised, because that *is* the power of raising your inner game.

Our inner game is our inner life—it's our thoughts, our emotions, and our physical state. And *raising* our inner game means strengthening our self-control in these areas. In other words, it's about developing what psychologists call *cognitive control, emotional self-regulation,* and *impulse control.* When you get right down to it, that's what this material helps you do, and those skills go right to the heart of who we are and what we're capable of. So it's no surprise that, as we get stronger in these areas, we automatically become more effective at whatever else we want to do. Your dream might not be to lose weight or get your Ph.D., but I'm sure there's *something* in your life that you want to improve, or you wouldn't have picked up this book.

In any case, over the next two years, the program went through several more iterations (an eight-week, video-based, online course; a six-week version of that same course; and a half-day live workshop) until, finally, the time came when I felt that I'd learned enough about the material to write the book.

ON THE SHOULDERS OF GIANTS

I've said a lot now about me and what I've done to develop *Raise Your Inner Game*. And though I do believe it's important for you to hear my story and to know where the material came from, I don't want to give the impression that the book is *about* me, because it isn't at all. So, as the last thing before we begin, allow me to put my role here into perspective.

First, I haven't developed this material in a vacuum. I mentioned two influences already—Timothy Gallwey and Eckhart Tolle (whose work has been especially important)—but there have been many others as well: Sam Harris, Rudolf Steiner, and Lao Tzu, to name just a few. But more to the point, the observations at the core of this book are not things that I created, any more than I created the solar system.

They're objective, observable truths about the nature of the inner game. All I've done here is to create what I hope is an easier and more accessible guidebook, if you will—a way for you to discover and understand those truths for yourself, so that you can put them into action in your life.

Think of it this way: If I were your guide for a rafting trip through the Grand Canyon, the feelings of awe you'd experience during the trip wouldn't be because of *me*, they'd be because the Grand Canyon is awesome. In a similar way, if this book brings about the kind of change for you that it has for me and for others, it's not ultimately because of anything I've done; it's only because of the inherent power in the underlying truths of the inner game.

With that, let's get started.

PART ONE

THE INNER GAME

AND HOW IT WORKS

CHAPTER 1

THE INNER GAME FRAMEWORK

The purpose of Part One is to give you a new way to recog-nize and understand the workings of your inner game, because understanding it is what gives you the power to control it. To get started, imagine that your inner world is a building, with four stories, or levels, like this:

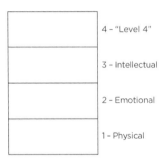

We're dividing what we might call your "total self" into four distinct parts, with Levels 1, 2, and 3 representing your physical, emotional, and intellectual aspects, and Level 4 representing what you can think of as "you at your best." It's your most insightful, clear-thinking, creative, energized self.

In addition to the four levels, there are two more elements to the model: an elevator, for moving between the levels, and *you*, standing off to the side. Put all three elements together, and you get this, the Inner Game Framework:

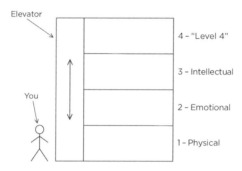

Four Levels, an Elevator, and You. This is the model we'll be working with from here on.

MORE THAN JUST A METAPHOR

We'll be discussing the Inner Game Framework in detail in the next chapters. But first I want to point out that this four-level pattern shows up in other interesting places; for example, in human behavior.

When people are at their worst, they can act in ways that are quite primitive and animal-like—defensive, aggressive, territorial, domineering, etc. This can be thought of as Level 1 behavior because it's driven by our most basic, physical, survival-oriented impulses. At the other end of the spectrum, when we're at our *best*, we are the complete opposite of our Level 1 selves, acting on our highest, most evolved impulses—generous, relaxed, open, caring, and so on, which can be thought of as being on Level 4. And most of the time, our behaviors are somewhere in between, on Levels 2 and 3. (More on all this in the next chapter.)

Another place you can see this four-level pattern is in our individual development from birth to adult. As infants, and for the first several years, we're in a physical-dominant stage (Level 1), meaning that we experience and learn primarily through our bodies—movement, sound, touch, and taste. In our middle childhood and teenage years, we become emotion-dominant (Level 2), and our primary focus becomes our community—friends, social groups, etc. Next, in early adulthood, we graduate into the intellect-dominant stage (Level 3), which means, among other things, that we can finally use reason to control our impulses and emotions. (We literally can't do this until this third stage, which explains a lot about high school.) And then finally, typically in our mid-40s, we experience a shift into what feels like a new, higher level of perception (Level 4), where we gain our fullest, deepest perspectives and insights into life. (By the way, this fourth stage is not always a happy shift. It's no coincidence that this is when midlife crises tend to happen. When people suddenly see things more deeply and clearly, it's not uncommon for them to look at their lives and think, "Wait, really? Is *this* what I wanted?" It can be a difficult period. On the other hand, this Level 4 shift is the reason grandparents tend to be better with young children—their new perspective helps them be more present and patient.)

You can even see the four levels in our brain anatomy and its "lower" and "higher" functions. The base of our brain, sometimes called the "reptilian brain," regulates basic physical systems (Level 1)—breathing, heart rate, hunger, etc. Next up is the *limbic system*, which is the center of emotional activity (Level 2), among other things. The large outer layer, the *cerebral cortex*, is associated with language, logic, and reason (Level 3: intellectual). And our highest, most advanced intellectual abilities, such as creativity, innovation, and insight, correspond with Level 4.

The point with these comparisons (besides that they're fascinating) is that this four-level framework is more than just a casual metaphor. It's a reasonable description of how we're actually put together, which is why thinking in these terms is so helpful in gaining control over your inner game.

YOU ARE SEPARATE FROM THE LEVELS

As simple as the Inner Game Framework is, it has much to tell us about how the inner game works—and we're going to get into all of that shortly. But you can see the most important lesson right now by simply looking at the model. And here it is:

You are separate from the levels.

It's not a hard concept to grasp, intellectually, that there's a *you* who is separate from the levels (if you can move between them, you are, by definition, separate from them). And, of course, that's what the above illustration shows. But this is the observation at the heart of raising your inner game. It was seeing and experiencing this that started all the changes in my life, and it's something you can easily observe for yourself as well, which brings us to the following exercise. (This is the first of the exercises I mentioned in the introduction. Please do it right now, if you can.)

EXERCISE: "YOU ARE NOT YOUR THOUGHTS."
Sit comfortably, relax, close your eyes, and, for a couple of minutes, observe your thoughts. Don't judge them or filter them, and try especially not to engage with them. Just watch them come and go, like you're sitting on a park bench and your thoughts are people walking by, or you're a birdwatcher peering through binoculars: "There's one! That's interesting. Hey, there's another." The approach you want is that of a distant but interested observer.

After you've observed your thought activity for a while, sit with the experience for a moment and feel the reality it demonstrates: On one hand are the thoughts you observed. On the other, there's *you* who observed them. They are separate things, like two people sitting on opposite sides of a table.

To put this another way, you *have* thoughts but you are *not* your thoughts (and, by extension, you have emotions but you are not your emotions, and you have a body but you are not your body).

Do you see it? Can you feel the *you*, separate from your thoughts? I hope so, because this is the reality that the Inner Game Framework shows: There's a *you* who's separate from the levels just as there's a *you* who's separate from your thoughts. And nothing gives you more power over your inner game than experiencing this simple truth for yourself.

CHAPTER 2

THE LEVELS

The Inner Game Framework illustrates the basic components of the inner game: the levels, the elevator, and *you*. But it doesn't tell us much about how the game actually *works*. For that, we need to take a closer look at each of the four levels and the role they play in our lives. There are three important points to understand and remember:

1. You're not on any one level all the time. You move between them, like you're on an elevator.
2. As you move between the levels, you change— so much so that you essentially "become" a different person.
3. The person you become is generally not someone you want to be.

A Level Story
It was New Year's Eve, and Margret and I had just dropped off our children at the babysitter's on the way to a party. As we walked back down the stairs, I landed

wrong on the bottom step and badly twisted my ankle. It isn't often you truly injure yourself, but when you do, you can tell. I instantly knew something was very wrong. I stood still for a few moments, and as I did, I could feel panic working through my body. Finally, with eyes wide and heart racing, I said to Margret, "I think I really hurt my ankle. What should we do? I'm not sure I can get to the car. *But I really want to go home!*"

This is an example of what I mean when I say moving to a level turns you into a different person. With the injury, I moved to Level 1 (the physical-dominant state), and as I did, changed from someone who was open, enthusiastic, and looking forward to being with people (a typical Level 4 state) to essentially the complete opposite—frightened, negative, self-focused, and repelled by the thought of being with people.

Now, you could say, "Wait, you didn't turn into a different *person*. You just had a natural reaction to injuring yourself. Of course you felt that way." But let's take a closer look. When we think about who someone is as a person, our sense of them is typically based on characteristics such as their priorities and motivations, their perspective and worldview, their sense of humor and what interests them, and the way they move and hold themselves. Within a few moments of twisting my ankle, every one of these characteristics had changed for me, and dramatically. So, in a very real sense, I truly did become a different person. And remember, I'm not saying that I became a different person *permanently*, just that I did so *in that moment.* Also, this is an extreme example—a painful physical injury. Moving to a level is not usually that dramatic. But a similar change does happen every time, and it's very helpful to learn to recognize this process at work in your life.

Next, we'll delve into each of the levels individually, and the changes that happen as we move between them.

LEVEL 1: THE PHYSICAL LEVEL

This is the realm of sensory input and primitive, instinctive impulses. When we're on Level 1, these impulses take control of our thoughts and actions.

My ankle story is a good example. The moment I twisted it, I started feeling instinctive survival impulses —*protect, cover, isolate*—and all I wanted to do was go home. Other examples range from mild (you're so hungry you're crabby; so tired you can't keep your eyes open) to profound enough that you change into an almost subhuman state (blind rage, panic, an addict desperately searching for the next fix). In all these cases the mechanism is the same—a physical condition is dominating your thoughts and actions.

Level 1 also drives our appetites and compulsions. When you impulsively reach for a sweet or a smoke, or sneak a peek at a shapely body, you're being driven by this lowest, most primitive level. *Yum. Pretty. Want. Need.*

Interestingly, you might not consciously want whatever it is you're reaching for. You might even specifically want *not* to have it. But the unfortunate truth is, your conscious mind has very little control over Level 1 drives, as anyone trying yet another diet can tell you.

Before reading on, take a moment to reflect on your experience of Level 1:

- When have you been on this level?
  (Think of a specific instance or two.)
- What put you there? (What caused it?)
- What sort of person did it turn you into?
- How did you feel about yourself afterward?

LEVEL 2: THE EMOTIONAL LEVEL

When you're on Level 2, your emotions have taken charge, and all your thoughts and actions come from this nonlogical place. This is not to say there's anything wrong with emotions, of course. They're fundamental to who we are, allowing us to feel and to relate to others. The problem comes when you get so *consumed* by emotion that you say and do things you don't mean—and will almost certainly regret. "Emotional hijack" is another way to describe the Level 2 state, and the symptoms are being irrational and overdramatic.

A Level 2 Transformation

I'm not good at waiting in line. If it's taking very long at all, especially if it's longer than I *think* it should take, I can pretty quickly turn into a real jerk. *What in the world? What is* wrong *with you people? How can this possibly take this long? Do you know what you're doing? Do you see the impact you're having on the rest of us? Do you even* care*? It's ridiculous. Outrageous! You're idiots!*

Judgmental, arrogant, entitled, negative. It's embarrassing.

Fortunately, I generally do a good job of keeping these thoughts to myself; but still, they're not pretty.

This is another example of how being on a level turns us into a different person—and someone we generally don't want to be. Look at the change as I shift in and out of Level 2. When I'm in the heat of the moment, I genuinely mean everything I'm thinking. All that nasty stuff—I mean it all. But the moment I step back, I *don't* mean it. Not any of it. I have a completely different perspective. In fact, the perspective is so different, not only do I not mean it, *I'm embarrassed for having thought it in the first place.* "That's not me," I think. And on those rare occasions when I slip and let others see this behavior, they have the same reaction: "That's not you."

Jekyll and Hyde. Bruce Banner and The Hulk. You and your "That's not me" self. As you move to Level 2, or any other level, you truly do become a different version of yourself.

Some Level 2 reflection questions:

- When have you been on this emotional-hijack level?
- What caused it?
- What did you say and do?
- How did you feel about yourself afterward?
- What do you think of others when they act like that?

LEVEL 3: THE INTELLECTUAL LEVEL

When you're on Level 3, your logical, analytical self has taken over, and all your thoughts and actions are coming from that perspective. This may sound like a good thing, but it's generally not. In fact, as bad as it sounds to be on Levels 1 and 2, it's Level 3 that creates the most trouble in our lives, for two reasons.

"Checked Out"

The first and main problem with Level 3 has to do with being "checked out." If you've ever been at dinner and someone had to say "Hello?" to get your attention, or you've been driving and missed a turn because your thoughts were elsewhere, that's being checked out. It basically means you're off in your head somewhere—daydreaming, lost in thought—rather than paying attention to what's in front of you.

This is something I really have to watch out for, especially if I'm working on a new song. With "normal" writing (books, articles, etc.), it's not a problem. Ninety-nine percent of that work happens at the computer, and when an idea pops into my head from time to time, it's not a major distraction. But songwriting is a different story. Most of that work happens in my head, and when musical ideas are coming, they can really take over. In fact, my family can always tell when there's a new song in the works. ("Uh oh. There goes Dad again.") I'm like a robot whose switch has been turned off—my body is there, but in every other way I'm completely gone.

The important thing to know about this checked-out aspect of Level 3 is that (in a milder form) this is our *default state.* We pop in and out of the other levels, but Level 3 is where we live. Here's a dramatization to illustrate—a slice of a typical inner life, starting from Level 3:

> *Thinking about me.*
> *Thinking about you.*
> *Wondering what you're thinking about me.*
> *Thinking you're thinking I'm fat.*
> *Fat fat fat.*

Food food food.

Thinking thinking thinking.

[stub toe]

Ow!

[move to Level 1]

Ow! Ow!

Arrgh!

Wow, that hurts.

Oh, my goodness.

Pain.

Pain.

Thinking about pain.

Thinking about pain.

[back to 3]

Thinking about my dentist.

Thinking about my ex.

Thinking about my ex thinking about me.

Ex ex ex.

Thinking thinking thinking.

[check the news]

Oh, that's not good.

Don't like that.

Angry about that.

[move to Level 2]

Anger! Anger!

Hate! Hate!

Hate them! Hate them!

THE LEVELS

> *Thinking about them.*
> *Thinking about them.*

[back to 3 again]

> *Thinking about them thinking about me.*
> *Thinking what I'd say to them.*
> *Thinking what they'd say back.*
> *Thinking thinking thinking.*
> *Me, them, me.*

[step outside]

> *Wow!*
> *It's beautiful out here.*
> *The fresh air—it smells so great.*
> *I FEEL so great.*

[move to Level 4]

> *SO beautiful!*
> *I love it.*
> *LOVE it.*
> *Just standing here, loving it.*
> *Thinking about love.*
> *Thinking about love.*

[back to Level 3]

> *Thinking about my honey.*
> *Thinking my honey thinks I'm fat.*
> *Fat fat fat.*
> *Me me me.*

Here's the same sequence in graphic form:

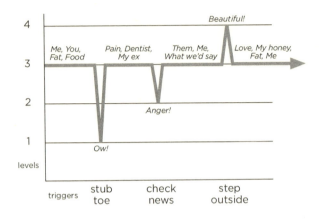

This is what the inner life is like for most people. We spend the vast majority of our time locked in an endless stream of mental noise just like this. We're not focused on the task at hand, not present with the people in our lives, and not working anywhere near our full potential.

This checked-out aspect of Level 3 can be hard to see because it's so much a part of our normal experience. But we need to learn to recognize and understand it— and ultimately control it—because this entanglement with Level 3 is the single biggest impediment to raising your inner game.

Level 3 entanglement is the single biggest impediment to raising your inner game.

No Empathy

The second problem associated with being on Level 3 is that when your logical self takes over, your emotional and physical selves get pushed to the background—you're not connected with them, not factoring them into your thoughts and actions. The effect of this is to essentially shut down your empathy.

Logic without empathy can lead to a wide range of bad behaviors because empathy is what helps us care about and connect with people, especially those who are different from us. So what kind of person does this logic-without-empathy state turn us into? Insensitive, cold, entitled, arrogant—and potentially much worse. And if you've ever known someone who fits that description, I don't need to tell you that this is not the kind of person you want to be.

Now, to be clear, I'm not saying *this* is our default state. We're not walking around being insensitive jerks all day (or at least most of us aren't). Nevertheless, when our emotional and physical selves get pushed to the background, it can quickly turn us into a particularly unappealing version of ourselves—and it happens more often than you might think.

Level 3 reflection questions:

- What are some examples of when you've been "checked out"?
- What problems did it create?

- When have you been insensitive, entitled, or arrogant?
- What do you think of people who fit that description?

LEVEL 4: YOU AT YOUR BEST

Open, relaxed, confident. Energized, creative, fully engaged and alive. Your thinking is clearer, you're more creative and insightful, and you make better decisions. You're more present with people—listening, connecting, and communicating better. This is what it's like on Level 4. It truly is, as I've said, you at your best. When you're on Levels 1, 2, and 3, you turn into someone you don't want to be, but your Level 4 self is *exactly* who you want to be. The goal of raising your inner game is to work and live from this highest level as much as possible.

The great news is that Level 4 is not some distant, hard-to-attain state. It's a normal part of everyday life that I expect you're familiar with already. Here are some typical ways people experience Level 4:

- Being outside in nature
- Spending time with young children
- Listening to music
- Laughter/humor

With each of these, you're not off in your head somewhere, lost in thought or worrying about something. You're just there in the moment, fully engaged in what you're doing. That's the essence of Level 4, and it's already part of your life. Imagine the difference, though, if rather than experiencing it in a few small moments here and there, you could work and live from there every day.

When you access Level 4, you open up the full measure of what you're capable of right now and in every moment. You're truly operating at your highest level, fully inhabiting your potential. At the same time, the state itself is profoundly simple: Your mind is quiet. You're not wrapped up in the mental noise of Level 3, the emotions of Level 2, or the physical impulses of Level 1.

> When you access Level 4, you open up the full measure of what you're capable of right now and in every moment.

It's difficult to communicate the full picture of Level 4 because there's such a contrast between the scope of the transformation and the simplicity of the state. But hopefully this gives you a good feel for it because, again, the goal is to operate from this highest level as much as possible.

Level 4 reflection questions:

- What are some Level 4 experiences you've had?
- What situations or activities trigger this level for you?
- How often do you have a Level 4 experience? (How many times per day/week?)
- How would you describe the feeling?
- How do you feel about yourself and your life when you're there?

Frequently Asked Level 4 Questions

When I'm talking with people about the four levels, a few questions consistently come up about Level 4, so I want to address those before we move on.

Q: Is Level 4 the same as being in a "flow" state?
A: Yes, in a way. But that doesn't mean a flow state is what we're working toward.

Flow is a very specific kind of Level 4 experience. It's when a basketball player, for example, gets "into the zone" (time slows down, he can see everything that's happening on the court and knows exactly what to do) or an artist gets so absorbed in her work that she loses all sense of time and place. Peak states like these *are*, technically, Level 4 states (your mind is quiet, you're fully engaged in what you're doing), but they occur in such rarified circumstances that they don't really apply to what we're talking about here.

If we get into a true flow state now and then, great. But raising your inner game is not about chasing peak experiences. It's about raising your current baseline to a higher level so you can do your best work and consistently feel engaged, energized, and fully alive.

> Raising your inner game is not about chasing peak experiences. It's about raising your current baseline to a higher level so you can do your best work and consistently feel engaged, energized, and fully alive.

Q: You say that when we're on Level 4, our thinking is clearer. But isn't thinking a Level 3 activity?
A: Actually, no. Thinking *is* intellectual in nature, but it occurs on all four levels.

When I twisted my ankle and moved to Level 1, I was still *thinking*, but my thoughts were coming from a more primitive, survival-based perspective (protect, cover, isolate: *I want to go home*). When I got upset while waiting in line, my thoughts were coming from an emotional, Level 2 perspective (*What is* wrong *with you people?*). So, we're thinking all the time, but the *nature* of our thoughts changes to reflect the perspective of whichever level we're on. (This is a big part of what makes it seem like you've become a different person—your thinking has changed.)

Q: If thinking occurs on all four levels, what makes Level 4 thinking different and/or better than thinking from the lower levels, if it is?
A: Oh, it's definitely better, and the reason has to do, again, with *perspective.*

Lower-level thinking, by definition, is limited to the narrow perspective of one particular level (survival drives on Level 1; emotions on Level 2; logic on Level 3). Level 4 thinking, on the other hand, takes *all* the levels into account, which makes for more insightful, higher-quality decisions.

As an example, say there's a performance issue with a co-worker—he or she is dropping the ball, not keeping up, and it's been going on for a while and seems to be getting worse. From a logic-only perspective (Level 3), it makes sense to think that the co-worker should be let go, and the sooner, the better. But when you move to Level 4 and look at the whole picture—a health crisis in the person's family, the emotional impact on the rest of the team, alignment with the company's values—it might make more sense to wait and offer the person support in turning things around. Both options make sense from within their relative perspectives, but the whole-picture, Level 4 analysis is better because it takes into account the full spectrum of information.

Now, I'm not suggesting it's always better in a situation like this to give someone more time. In a different situation, the full picture could suggest that making a change right away makes more sense. The point isn't about any one decision. It's to try to base *all* your decisions on full-spectrum thinking.

CHAPTER 3

THE ELEVATOR

Now that you understand the levels and the kind of person they turn you into (and that your Level 4 self is who you want to be), the last piece of the framework to talk about is the elevator. We learned earlier that we're not on any one level all the time; we move between them, like on an elevator. Here's how that works:

With a normal elevator, if you want to go to a different floor, you push the corresponding button. The inner elevator is different. For one thing, there are no buttons. For another, we're not in control! Who *is* in control? *The levels.* The inner elevator is directly controlled by the levels themselves.

To picture how this works, think of each level as having its own powerful magnet. When a level gets triggered, its magnet pulls you to that level. You're hungry, for example—a physical trigger. That activates your Level 1 magnet, the pull kicks in, and down you go to Level 1. You get upset—an emotional trigger. On comes your Level 2 magnet, and off you go to Level 2.

And it's the same with all four levels—when a level gets triggered, it pulls you to it.

To illustrate, think about a terrible customer-service experience you've had, the worst one you can think of. Take yourself back to that moment. Picture everything that happened, every stupid thing the other person said, every feeling you felt. Make it as complete a memory as possible. So, now you're feeling angry, right? That's the inner elevator in action. The memory triggered your emotions and pulled you to Level 2.

Here's another illustration. Take thirty seconds and see if you can answer this question: *What color was your bedroom painted when you were in the sixth grade?* The question pulls you off into your head. You call up images, trying to remember. Those images bring up other thoughts that pull you off into them—and now you're on Level 3.

The important point here is that you're not normally doing this yourself. The levels do it *to* you. The reality is, most of the time, for most people, we're not in control of our inner state. We don't decide which level we're on or which version of ourselves we're being from one moment to the next. We're just along for the ride, getting pulled around by our lower levels.

It's sort of depressing to realize, but it is the truth.

The good news is that's all about to change. By reading this book, you're learning how to take control of your state in ways you never could before.

EXERCISE: LEVEL REPORT

We've just seen two illustrations of the elevator in action. Take a few minutes now to think about other examples of this process at work in your life.

In the past forty-eight hours:

- What levels were you on, and when?
  (Think of examples of all four.)
- For each level, what was the trigger? In other words, what was the thought, feeling, or physical condition that caused you to move to that particular level?

CHAPTER 4

INNER GAME MOMENTS

Here's what we know so far about the inner game and how it works:

1. There are four levels, which represent the four aspects of your total self.
2. You are separate from the levels and move between them, like on an elevator.
3. As you do, you turn into different versions of yourself.
4. The levels themselves are what pull you from one level to another.

The last element to point out is that this whole process of moving between the levels plays out in tiny moments that happen throughout your day. A feeling of hunger, a flash of anger, an idea popping into your mind each occur in a moment. This might seem so obvious that it's not worth mentioning, but the truth is, the reason people so frequently struggle with their inner game is precisely because they don't pay attention to these moments. *This is where the game is played.* It's in these moments that we turn into the person we don't want to be.

Moment Stories

I was out on a run one day. It was a typical run for me—a half-hour long, three miles. At one point, I came around a bend and noticed, about 100 feet ahead, a basketball in the street. It was in my way and also in the way of any cars that might come by.

My first thought was pretty straightforward: *Kick the ball into the yard as you go by.* Easy to do. Good thing to do. Helps everybody out. Not a controversial idea. But, *Hmm*, I started thinking, *maybe the ball doesn't belong to that house.*

I don't know whose ball it is. Can't assume it's theirs.

Might not be polite to kick a strange ball into someone's yard.

It's certainly not my responsibility to do it, right? It's not my ball. I didn't put it there.

Meanwhile, even at my pace, 100 feet goes by pretty quickly. So the next thing I knew, I was three steps past the ball—and still the debate continued: *What now? Do I go back? Seriously? Stop and turn around, just to kick the ball out of the way? Is it that big a deal? You know, I'm on a run here. Things to do. Gotta get home.* And on it went.

It was a classic Inner Game Moment.

Another example: I'm in a restaurant, deciding what to drink with my meal. My plan is to have water. Water's good. I like water. A Coke sounds pretty good, too, to be honest, but I'm trying to avoid soda. So, OK, good. Got a plan. *Water with lunch.*

The server comes. "Something for you to drink, sir?"

"Yeah… I'll have a Coke, please."

What happened?! Another Inner Game Moment.

THE LEVELS AT WORK

These moments go by so fast that we don't realize what's happening. But if you slow the tape down, you can clearly see what's going on: It's the levels at work.

Take my basketball story. First, I got the idea to kick the ball out of the street, and then I immediately started hearing arguments against it. *Maybe it's not theirs. It's not my job. Not worth the trouble,* and so on. That was Level 3, making intellectual arguments. I was also seeing pictures in my mind of the homeowners looking stern and judgmental because I'd kicked a stranger's ball into their yard. That was Level 2 creating an emotional pull. Finally, like momentum against a turning ship, I felt a subtle, and unconscious, physical pull against the whole idea, which was, of course, Level 1. It all happened in an instant, but all three levels came together to oppose my idea, and it worked. I ran right on by.

This is what happens in Inner Game Moments. They don't always involve all three levels, but the mechanism is the same: You feel a magnet's pull in a moment, and you either go along with it or you don't. Go with it, you lose. Resist it, you win.

That's the game. And seeing this clearly can truly change your life. Now let's experience it in real time.

EXERCISE: INNER GAME MOMENTS

In this exercise you're going to create an Inner Game Moment and observe this mechanism at work. It's a very specific exercise, so please follow the instructions to the letter. And as you do it, remember that the purpose is to observe what happens in these moments.

1. Note the current time.
2. Identify the next ten-minute mark. (If it's 2:12 now, the next mark will be 2:20. If it's 7:31, it'll be 7:40, and so on.)
3. Think of some small action you could do at that time (e.g., check your email, call someone, take a deep breath).
4. As you wait, note any pull against taking that action—arguments, physical impulses, etc.
5. When the ten-minute mark comes, take action at precisely that moment.

Steps 3 and 5 are especially important: The action needs to be small and relatively unimportant, and you need to do it at *exactly* the ten-minute mark—not one second before or after. (I know this may sound a bit extreme, but trust me, the precision is important. And, by the way, the pull you're feeling right now against doing all this is part of the exercise. Don't let it beat you!)

"WHO WAS SAYING THAT?"

The first time I did an exercise like this, I set out to make my bed at 7:35 a.m. every day for a week, and I was amazed by how difficult it was to actually follow through and do it, and at the arguments that came up against it. Sometimes I would get distracted by something and forget it altogether. When I did remember, there was always pressure to do it before the specified time: *It doesn't matter if you do it a minute early. This is stupid. Just do it now. You're wasting time.*

This has become one of my favorite exercises, for a couple of reasons. First, it's a perfect demonstration of the inner game in action. You can see every element we've talked about at work: the levels pulling at you; the different kinds of arguments and opposition they generate—physical, emotional, and intellectual; the feelings associated with going along or resisting. It's all there, and it's very helpful to be able to experience it so clearly for yourself.

The other reason I love this exercise is that it's a direct and powerful experience of you being separate from the levels. Think again about my bed-making story and the arguments I heard as the time approached—*It doesn't matter. This is stupid. Do it now. You're wasting time.*

Who was saying that? And why would he care?

When you get into a moment like this, debating your lower levels, it's almost as if there's an actual person standing there arguing with you, with his or her own ideas about what you should and shouldn't do. The difference between the two of you is just so clear and tangible.

I can't stress enough how important and valuable it is to recognize this difference. Remember, this is the core observation of the inner game: There's something else *in there*, in your inner world, that's working against you. And that's why it's so important to do these exercises. The more clearly you experience this for yourself, the more power you'll have over your inner game.

CHAPTER 5

INNER GRAVITY

You now have the full picture of how your inner game works. You have the structure (the levels, the elevator, and you), you understand the mechanism (the levels pull you to them), and finally, you know it all happens in Inner Game Moments, where you feel a level's pull and you either go along with it or resist.

The last idea to cover before moving on to Part Two is *gravity*.

A SIMPLER PICTURE

When managing my inner game, I don't normally think about all the details we've discussed so far—levels, triggers, etc. I do think about them when I'm trying to analyze a particular problem and figure out the best way to deal with it. But holding the full picture in your mind all the time isn't practical, or even necessary. From here on out, I suggest you think of your inner game much more simply. First, use the word "gravity" as shorthand for all the pull and struggle from our lower levels. Then take everything we've talked about in Part One and condense it down to this:

- You're trying to operate from Level 4.
- Gravity's trying to pull you down.
- You're trying to keep that from happening by resisting the pull.

Understanding the full picture is important, especially as you're getting started; but most of the time, this simpler picture is all the detail you'll need.

Why *Gravity*?

First of all, as with physical gravity, the pull of inner gravity is a natural force. With all the talk of you being separate from the levels and there being "something else in there" working against you, it can sound like I'm saying you've been taken over by a foreign invader. (And the truth is, it can *feel* like that at times.) But of course, as we've said, the pull is just our lower levels doing what they do. It's a natural part of life.

Second, it's a *downward* force, and there's no question about that. Inner gravity pulls us toward our lower levels and works against our positive intentions. Steven Pressfield writes powerfully about this in his book *The War of Art*—he calls it "Resistance"—and you can see it in your own life every day. It doesn't matter what you're trying to do; you'll feel gravity's pull against it.

Third, it's always there. The intensity varies from day to day, but the pull never goes away, and never will. This is an important point. The goal in raising your inner game is not to make gravity go away, because that's simply not possible. The goal is to learn to rise above it.

The goal in raising your inner game is not to make gravity go away, it's to learn to rise above it.

GRAVITY VARIES

Another helpful observation about inner gravity is that it varies. Physical gravity doesn't, of course. Its pull is constant. But inner gravity varies from day to day and from moment to moment.

Have you ever had days that seem harder for no apparent reason—you're not short of sleep, sick, or anything else you can put your finger on—you just feel heavier, like everything's uphill? Those are high-gravity days. And then some days are exactly the opposite. You feel light, capable, naturally at ease, like a weight has been lifted, again for no apparent reason. Those are low-gravity days.

High-Gravity Conditions

In addition to the natural fluctuations of inner gravity, certain conditions can increase this downward pull. If you hurt your back, for example, and are dealing with chronic pain, it's very difficult to have the energy and focus you want. A workshop attendee who was eight months pregnant once said, "I am definitely having some high-gravity days," and I can only imagine how right she was. It's a perfect example.

Another high-gravity condition is when there's something you can't stop obsessing about. For me this typically happens when I'm consumed with a creative project, or when I'm upset or worried about something. Whatever the cause, it makes it very difficult to stay up on Level 4 where I want to be.

High-Gravity Triggers

Not only does gravity vary on its own and under certain conditions, but there are objects, situations, and even people that trigger your lower levels, causing a sharp increase in your inner gravity.

Television is a great example of a high-gravity trigger. It's just about impossible to resist looking at a TV when it's on. And if you've ever observed others while they watch, especially children, there's no doubt that it's pulling them to a lower level.

The donut case at the local convenience store can be a high-gravity trigger (speaking here from personal experience). With my sweet tooth, I feel the pull every time I walk by.

Certain jobs or positions can be high-gravity triggers. If someone's in a job that's a bad fit, their performance and happiness will both suffer.

News sources—online, radio, TV, take your pick—are powerful high-gravity triggers. (Sadly, this is by design. Emotions, especially negative ones, are good for their business.)

People can be the biggest high-gravity triggers of all. Negative, angry, sarcastic, cynical, needy, boring, complaining, lazy—some people radiate their lower-level energy so powerfully that they're like mini black holes, with a pull so massive nothing can escape, including you.

A POWERFUL INNER GAME STRATEGY

The point here is that, as you become aware of variations in gravity and the high-gravity conditions and triggers in your life, you can start to make adjustments to manage them. If it's a high-gravity day, you can up your inner game to keep from getting pulled down (using the skills and tools you'll learn in Part Two). With high-gravity triggers, you can work to avoid and remove them from your life. Which approach is better will depend on the particular situation. But learning to recognize and manage your inner gravity is a powerful strategy for mastering your inner game.

EXERCISE: GRAVITY REPORT

Think back over the past three days:

- Were they high-gravity, low-gravity, or normal days?
- How can you tell? What do the differences feel like?
- What high-gravity triggers did you encounter?
- What other high-gravity triggers can you identify in your life?

CHAPTER 6

SUMMARY, PART ONE

Before you know how your inner game works, the whole thing is just one big mystery, and it's very difficult to have any consistent control over it. But once you understand the mechanism (it's your lower levels pulling you around in these tiny Inner Game Moments), the solution becomes obvious: You simply need to start paying attention to these moments and resist the pull.

Of course, understanding that isn't *all* you need. You still have to figure out how to do it (which is where the skills and tools in Part Two come in), and then you have to put what you've learned into action. But understanding is the critical first step, and you've taken that step now.

As a reminder, here are the main takeaways from Part One:

1. You are separate from the levels.
2. The Inner Game Framework and how it all works (the levels, the elevator, and the inner game moments).

3. Level 4—what it feels like when you're there and what it represents in your life. (Pages 34-39)
4. The simplified picture of your inner game. (Pages 49-50)

If you can keep these four core elements in mind as you go forward, they'll be a big help in doing the daily work of raising your inner game. So, before you go on, please take a moment to think through these takeaways. Sit with each idea. For those that feel clear, affirm that feeling: "Yes. I see that." For those that aren't as clear, review the relevant chapters, do the exercises, and keep thinking about them until they are. The more real and alive all this becomes for you, the bigger the change you'll be able to make in your life.

Now it's time to talk about the inner game skills and tools.

PART TWO

INNER GAME SKILLS AND TOOLS

CHAPTER 7

A PICTURE OF THE GOAL

In the next chapters, we're going to cover the skills and tools you need to raise your inner game. First, though, I want to give you a clear visual of what that means, so you can really understand what you're working toward. You know you want to operate from Level 4, but what does that look like? How will things be different from what's happening now? The following is a great way to picture it.

BE THE CEO OF YOUR INNER COMPANY

Think of your inner world as a business, with you as the CEO and your lower levels (1-3) as VPs of their different departments. There's a VP of Body, a VP of Emotions, and a VP of Brain. Each VP has his or her own perspective and opinion. They're all smart, valuable team members. You love them and genuinely appreciate their input. The only thing is: *You don't want them to be in charge*, which is how it works now. When a level gets triggered and pulls you to it, that's a VP being in charge, and it's a bad system. If your body gets to decide whether or not you drink a Coke, you're going to have the Coke. Every time. If your emotions are in charge of what you say, you're going to say things you regret. If your VP of Brain is dictating what you think about and when, you're going to be tangled up in Level 3 (again!)—checked out, distracted, negative, lost in the mental noise. It's when your VPs are in charge that you get pulled down and turned into someone you don't want to be.

How do you avoid it? Step up and take on the executive role—be the CEO of your inner company. You listen to your lower levels, you appreciate their input, but *you* decide what you do and say and think in any given moment.

That's what it looks like to operate from Level 4.

> You listen to your lower levels and appreciate their input, but *you* decide what you do and say and think in any given moment.

By the way, this corresponds perfectly with the three self-control skills I mentioned in the introduction—*cognitive control, emotional self-regulation*, and *impulse control*. Those are simply the technical terms for what we're talking about here—keeping your VPs of Brain, Emotions, and Body (respectively) from taking charge. (We'll be talking more about these three types of self-control in the coming chapters.)

CHAPTER 8

"NO. QUIET."

As I mentioned earlier, entanglement with Level 3 is the single biggest impediment to raising your inner game. This first skill, "No. Quiet," is how you break free of that entanglement. The idea is, when you notice the voice in your head (Level 3) pulling you down or off track, you simply say, "No. Quiet," and keep your thoughts where you want them instead.

It's difficult to overstate the difference this simple skill can make.

COGNITIVE CONTROL

The first type of self-control is *cognitive control*, which is the ability to intentionally point your attention to where you want it rather than have it go wherever *it* wants. Cognitive control is one of the most important and valuable skills you can have, and it's essential to being your best, both mentally and physically. In fact, in his book *Focus,* Daniel Goleman, the famed psychologist and author of *Emotional Intelligence,* calls cognitive control *the* fundamental success competency, even more fundamental than emotional intelligence.

All other competencies grow from it, or shrink in its absence.

When you say "No. Quiet" to the voice in your head, you're practicing—and developing—cognitive control.

Creativity

Cognitive control also has a profound impact on your creativity and your ability to access your best ideas. Think of it like this: When the water of a pond is agitated, light reflects off the rough surface, keeping you from seeing what's underneath. It's only when the water is still that you can see into the depths. Similarly, when you're wrapped up in the busyness and noise of your thoughts (Level 3 entanglement), your thinking is limited to the surface, so your observations tend to be obvious and uninspired.

To get to your deepest, most creative ideas, you have to quiet the noise. Cognitive control is how you do that, and "No. Quiet" is how you develop cognitive control. In fact, it's one of only two ways I'm aware of to do it. (We'll talk about the other in Chapter Ten.)

Insight and Intuition

This "seeing into the depths" effect doesn't apply only to creativity. It also gives you new and valuable insights into yourself and others, because you're able to perceive subtle information that is otherwise obscured by mental noise.

Here are just a few examples of the benefits of this enhanced insight and intuition:

- You develop a more nuanced sense of other people, so you can understand them more deeply and engage with them more effectively.
- You're more attuned to subtle changes in your own inner state, which helps you self-regulate with greater precision and operate at an even higher level.
- You're able to pick up subtle cues from your subconscious mind that alert you to opportunities and risks that others miss.

EMOTIONAL SELF-REGULATION

The second type of self-control is *emotional self-regulation*, and, in some ways, this is an even more helpful skill to develop than cognitive control, because our emotions have so much power over us.

Consider this scenario: Something's gone wrong. Maybe someone's made a mistake, and it's created a problem that needs to be dealt with. At first, it's frustrating, but you're fine—you're dealing with the problem rationally. But the more you think about it the more upset you get, until suddenly your frustration has boiled over into anger and you're saying things you'll regret.

Maybe this has never happened to you, and you've only seen it in others. But this is the kind of power that emotions have over your inner game. And here again, "No. Quiet" can help. When you notice negative thoughts pulling you somewhere you don't want to go, you simply say "No, thank you," and bring yourself back to where you want to be.

DEALING WITH PROBLEMS AND DISTRACTIONS

Typically, when a problem comes up in our work and lives, it immediately becomes a distraction. Regardless of whatever else we were doing, our thoughts become consumed by the new problem. (Which, by the way, is a perfect illustration of our VP of Brain being in charge—*it* is deciding what we're thinking about.) Cognitive control helps you deal more effectively with situations like this, because it enables you to shut down the internal dialogue rather than be distracted by it.

Am I suggesting that you should ignore problems when they come up? Not at all. If there's a legitimate issue, of course you need to deal with it. But you should do it *when it works for you,* not when your big brain thinks you should. Remember, you are CEO of your inner company, so that decision is *yours* from now on.

Now, I should point out that the vast majority of so-called problems your brain wants to talk about are *not* important. Think back to the illustration of a typical inner life from Chapter Two: *Thinking about me. Thinking about you. Thinking you're thinking I'm fat. Thinking about food. Yum. Hungry. Thinking about my dentist, and my ex. Thinking about that guy I hate. What he said. What I'd say to him. What he thinks about me.* Most of the thoughts our brain generates are childish, petty noise just like this, which don't deserve our attention. But even when a problem *is* important, being distracted by it all day long while you're trying to do other things doesn't do you or anyone else any good. It keeps you from being present with the work in front of you and the people around you. And, ironically, it *doesn't solve the problem*, because you're not giving the new issue your full attention, either.

Simply put, getting distracted like this is *not* owning the problem; it's letting the problem own *you*.

Here's the better way to go. First, plan a time to think about the issue. Look at your calendar, carve out some quality focus time, and make an appointment with yourself. Then, when your brain brings it up in the meantime ("Hey, let's think about *this!*"), you say, "No, not now. It can wait. I hear you. I agree, it's important. But it's on the calendar. We'll deal with it then."

That's operating from Level 4.

Remember, the goal is for *you* to decide what you think about and when. Or, as the Zen saying so beautifully puts it, "Be master *of* mind rather than mastered *by* mind."

SIMPLE YET POWERFUL

Don't let the simplicity of "No. Quiet" fool you. This is a powerful skill. In fact, this is the one that made the difference for Bridget, whose story I told in the introduction. Even though Bridget was already well-versed in other self-improvement programs, it was learning how to shut down the conversations in her head that ultimately led to her losing 58 pounds and earning her Ph.D. Your goals, I'm sure, are different from hers. But, like her, "No. Quiet" may well be the skill that makes them happen.

This is also where we start to see the practical effect of learning about the Inner Game Framework. When you understand, and better yet, when you've *experienced* that you are separate from the levels, it makes perfect sense to turn to your "other" self and ask it to be quiet. But when you don't see that separation, it's difficult to grab hold of the idea, and so you remain at the mercy of your lower levels.

The ultimate power in your inner game comes from being able to separate yourself from your thoughts, emotions, and physical state. When you can step back from your lower levels, you gain control over yourself. When you can't step back, the levels control you. So this is something you can (and should) start practicing right away. Watch for times when your thoughts or emotions are pulling you off track, resist the pull, and feel the difference this simple yet powerful skill makes.

CHAPTER 9

LIFTS

This next skill is a bit more advanced, but it's my favorite inner game tool. It's called a *Lift*, and I say it's advanced for two reasons. First, Lifts deal with such small moments they're almost invisible, so it can sometimes take a little longer to really understand how they work. Second, whereas the previous skill, "No. Quiet," is for tackling specific inner game issues like distractions and creativity, a Lift is purely about *being present and mindful in the moment*. We haven't talked about this idea yet (that's coming later in this chapter), but it goes right to the heart of what it means to operate from Level 4.

So, what is a Lift?

The best way to describe a Lift is with an example, so let's look again at my basketball-in-the-street story from Part One. If you remember, I noticed the ball in the road, meant to kick it out of the way, but got lost in gravity's pull and ran right past it. What I didn't tell you is that I ultimately did stop, went back, and kicked the ball out of the road—and it felt great.

That's a Lift. It's a little inner game "win" that brings with it a distinct uplifting feeling. Some other examples:

- Walking through the office, you notice a scrap of paper on the floor. Your first thought is to pick it up, but then you feel some inner opposition to doing it. You pick it up anyway, and now have a little more bounce in your step.
- You're on a run. You feel an impulse to stop and rest (*tired*), but you resist and continue—and you're suddenly less tired than you thought you were.
- You walk past a bowl of chips on the counter. Without even thinking about it, you reach out to grab one, but you catch yourself and pull your hand back, and feel surprisingly good about it.
- You're about to make some toast when you realize that you always put the first slice on the right side (no particular reason, that's just what you do), so you put it on the left instead and, for some reason, feel happier than you did a moment before.

The important thing to note here (because this is the part that trips people up) is just how small each of these moments is. And by *small*, I don't mean brief (all

Inner Game Moments are brief). I mean they're *low-gravity* moments, where there's very little at stake in the choice that's in front of you.

LIFTS REQUIRE LOW-GRAVITY MOMENTS

The purpose of doing a Lift is to "wake up," if you will, and be present in the moment. But if you try to do that with moments where the pull is too strong, it's not going to work—you're not going to be able to overcome the opposing force.

Look at the difference between the basketball story and the other Inner Game Moment I shared, which was when I ordered a Coke, even though I was planning on having water. The basketball instance was a low-gravity moment because it didn't really matter to me what I did. Kicking it out of the way seemed like a good thing to do, but it was not a big deal either way. The Coke, on the other hand, *was* a big deal. I have a strong craving for Coke, as you know, bordering on an addiction. So the pull toward having one is very strong, and there are complex issues involved in whether or not I give in to that pull. The result of this difference was that, in the low-gravity moment with the basketball, the Lift worked, but in the high-gravity moment with the Coke, it didn't. This is why it's so important for Lifts to be done with low-gravity moments: A Lift will only work when you use an Inner Game Moment that you can easily win.

WHY LIFTS GIVE YOU A LIFT

On first glance, it's not obvious why Lifts would feel so good (they're surprisingly, well, uplifting). But the reason has to do with the difference between acting *intentionally* and acting *unconsciously*.

When you go along with the pull you feel in an Inner Game Moment, you're acting unconsciously—sleepwalking, in a sense. You're being controlled by your lower levels, like a puppet on a string. And, no surprise, when you're in that unconscious state, the experience has a sort of sleepy, heavy quality to it (though you don't necessarily notice that while you're there). On the other hand, when you resist the pull and act intentionally, you wake up and rise to Level 4, which feels very alive and open and energized. So the reason Lifts are uplifting is simply that it feels better to wake up. (I'm exaggerating the differences here a bit for the purpose of the illustration, but it's a difference you can definitely feel, especially as you become more attuned to the variations in your inner state—which is what naturally happens as you spend more time working on your inner game.)

The Perfect Pick-Me-Up

This uplifting effect also makes Lifts the perfect tool for keeping you positive and engaged throughout your day. Next time you find yourself in a funk of some sort—crabby, dragging, feeling low—look for three or four of these little, low-gravity moments and do some Lifts, and you'll snap right out of it.

IMPULSE CONTROL

Beyond their waking-up effect and the feelings that come from that, the other important thing Lifts do for you is help develop the third type of self-control, *impulse control*. Most Inner Game Moments, especially the small ones we're talking about here, start as tiny, unconscious impulses—to order a Coke, to check your phone, to buy that shiny new object (it's on sale!). And every time you resist one of those impulses, you strengthen your ability to control *all* of your impulses.

THE POINT: WHO'S IN CHARGE

Given how small Lift moments need to be, it's easy to wonder if they really matter. And, in fact, by definition, low-gravity moments *don't* matter, not really. A ball in the street, a scrap of paper on the floor, which slot you use in the toaster—none of them matter in the larger scheme of things. But whether the act itself is important or not is the wrong question. From the perspective of your inner game, it's not what you're doing that matters most, but *why you're doing it*. Or, stated differently, *who's in charge*.

Raising your inner game ultimately and always comes down to this simple question: Right now, in this moment, are *you* in control or is gravity? If *you're* in control, you're awake, present, and operating from Level 4. If gravity's in control, you're sleepwalking and not working at your full potential. In every Inner Game Moment, no matter how small, that's the real choice you're making, and which path you choose makes all the difference in the world.

The paradox of Lifts is that these tiny moments can be so profoundly important in our lives, but that's the reality of the inner game.

Raising your inner game ultimately and always comes down to this simple question: Right now, in this moment, are *you* in control or is gravity?

So, those are Lifts—the Ninja moves of your inner game. Small. Quick. Almost invisible. But remarkably powerful. The sooner you can make these a part of your daily life, the better. (I'll show you a proven way to do that in Chapter Eleven.)

CHAPTER 10

FOCUSED SITTING

Now it's time to talk about a wonderful exercise called Focused Sitting, which is arguably your most important inner game tool.

The exercise itself is quite simple. You sit comfortably with your eyes closed and hands resting in your lap, and settle yourself into a nice, quiet state—alert, present, still. Then, as thoughts come up, which they will do almost immediately, you gently but firmly direct them to be still. It's essentially what you do with "No. Quiet," but in a controlled environment. (By the way, this alert, present state is also a pure Level 4 state: *Your mind is quiet.* More on that in a moment.) So you start from this quiet state, the thoughts pull you to Level 3, and you pull yourself back. *No, thank you. Quiet. Just sitting.* And this continues for the length of the exercise. Back and forth. Back and forth. Back and forth. Spending as much time as possible alert and present, and as little as possible on Level 3.

When you're in this quiet, Level 4 state, you're simply aware of what's going on around you, observing your senses and surroundings—the voice in the next room, the pressure of your back against the chair, the sensation of your hands in your lap, the air moving in and out of your lungs, the patterns of light behind your eyelids. You're not thinking about any of it, just observing. You also feel very awake and alive, especially compared with when you've drifted off into your thoughts. And I don't mean this metaphorically. When I drift off to Level 3, it feels like I'm dreaming. When I come back it feels like I'm waking up. (I can't help but wonder if this is where the weighty, spiritual metaphor of "waking up" came from in the first place—just someone a long time ago having this experience and trying to explain the feeling: "Well... um... it's like... *waking up*!") In any case, that's the basic exercise, and it's exactly what I do most mornings. For fifteen minutes, you simply sit, present and alert; and when gravity pulls you to Level 3, you gently but firmly pull yourself back.

(Here's a little tip to help with this: It's very common, when you pull yourself back from a thought, to slip back into that same train of thought. But if you silently *say the name* of what you're thinking about, it helps keep that from happening. For example, if you find yourself thinking about an upcoming meeting, saying "No *meeting*. Quiet," will work better than just saying "No. Quiet.")

The Visualization Option

Some people find that visualization helps them with Focused Sitting. Here's how that option works: First, you think up an imaginary scene that represents the basic dynamic of Focused Sitting (you, in charge, directing your thoughts), and then, rather than simply sitting and observing your sensory experience, you sit and visualize the scene. For example, you might imagine that you're a king or queen, sitting on your throne. Your advisors are in the room with you—ministers of Body, Emotions, and Brain—but for the moment, you're simply sitting and enjoying the silence. Now and then, one of them speaks up: "Pardon, your majesty?" and when they do, you turn to them and say, "No, not now. It can wait," and you return to the silence. Or you could picture yourself sitting on your front porch, enjoying the sun on your face, with your dog lying at your feet. When the dog sits up or gets restless, you say, "No, not now. Lie down." Any scene can work for this, as long as it has the essential elements: some kind of distraction to represent your thoughts, and you, directing those distractions to be still.

THE BENEFITS OF FOCUSED SITTING
Strengthens Your Willpower
The back and forth, tug-of-war of this exercise—you're pulled off into a thought, you pull yourself back—is very effective at building willpower.

Will is the force you use to pull yourself back—you're *exerting* your preference, *insisting* on silence, *willing* yourself back. So, each time you do it, it's like you're lifting a weight, strengthening your willpower muscle. Now, this is potentially true with every Inner Game Moment. Each time you resist the pull from any of the lower levels, you're exercising your will; and the more you do it, the stronger you get. But because Focused Sitting is so purely focused on this fundamental tug-of-war, it's like a Nautilus machine, perfectly designed to strengthen that muscle.

Accelerates Development of Cognitive Control
I mentioned earlier that the "No. Quiet" skill is one of two main ways to develop cognitive control. Focused Sitting is the other way, and it's actually the better option. When you're doing this exercise, you're simply sitting and directing your attention—it wanders, and you guide it back, again and again.

In other words, it's pure cognitive control practice.

With any skill, when you isolate the core activity and repeat it, you get better and stronger more quickly, and it's the same with this.

Helps Incorporate Level 4 Into Your Life
The normal experience of Level 4 comes as the result of a Level 4 trigger of some sort (being outdoors, listening to music, being with young children, etc.). Level 4 triggers themselves feel great and bring out all the positive traits we talked about, but since the experience is wrapped up in an activity, you don't get much

connection with the state itself. When you experience Level 4 as part of Focused Sitting, though, it's pure. There's nothing else going on. Just you, sitting, silent and alert, your mind quiet. So your connection with the state is very clear and direct, which makes Level 4 real for you in a way that nothing else does.

There are many benefits to this: It keeps you in touch with how alive you can feel when you're at your best, and with the kind of person you're capable of being; it motivates you to continue to grow and improve so that you can operate from that highest level more consistently; it provides encouragement when you're feeling down, and helps keep the lows from getting too low. But the most important, practical benefit has to do with the idea expressed in the pond metaphor that I mentioned earlier (you can see into the depths of things only when the water is calm). The quiet you experience in this exercise *is* that calm water. It's here that you find your most creative ideas. Now, I don't mean that you'll find them *while* you're doing Focused Sitting (the exercise is about quieting your thoughts, not engaging with them). What I'm suggesting is that operating at your highest level comes from learning to *incorporate* this Level 4 stillness into your regular activities. Meaning, being able to access this calm, quiet state when you're *not* doing the exercise, but just going about your daily life.

For example, when you're stuck on a problem, rather than continuing to struggle along the same line of thought, you step back, quiet your thoughts, and see what fresh ideas come up. Or, in a conversation, instead of jumping in with the first thing that comes to mind, you pause, get quiet, and consider how to respond effectively to what's been said. This is what it's like to incorporate Level 4 into your regular activities. It truly is the key to operating at your highest, most creative level, and the more time you spend experiencing this pure Level 4 state, the easier it is to do.

Operating at your highest level comes from learning to incorporate Level 4 into your regular activities.

Upgrades Your Brain

Perhaps the most significant thing Focused Sitting does for you is that it actually changes your brain, and in a profoundly positive way.

In the past few years, brain researchers have been able to show the physiological effects of mental exercises like Focused Sitting, and they're truly remarkable: increased gray matter cells in areas that control self-regulation, learning, and problem solving; decreased volume and influence of the amygdala (the brain's "fight or flight" center); and decreased activation of the default-mode network, which contributes to stilling the random chatter of the mind. All of this helps you be more calm, lowers your stress, makes you more emotionally resilient, raises the quality of your thinking and creativity, and helps you be more present and focused. In other words, this exercise takes all the traits we're working to bring out through raising your inner game and *builds them into your system,* giving a massive boost to your efforts.

THE (NOT-SO) SECRET WEAPON OF ELITE PERFORMERS

As if all that weren't enough, here's one more reason to make this exercise a part of your daily life: Champions and elite-level performers in all walks of life are already doing it.

Focused Sitting is a form of meditation (specifically, of *Vipassana* meditation: a continued close attention to sensation, thoughts, and feelings), and meditation of one kind or another is a habit that a striking percentage of high-level performers have in common. Athletes, artists, entrepreneurs, soldiers, actors, CEOs, journalists, doctors, investment bankers, world leaders—the list goes on. And the reason they do it is because they know that a mental exercise like this is an indispensable part of operating at their highest level.

"I'M NOT VERY GOOD AT IT"

The first thing most people say after they try Focused Sitting is, "I'm not very good at it," by which they mean their thoughts aren't getting quiet and the exercise is a bit of a struggle, rather than being the peaceful experience they expected. The feelings are certainly understandable, but if *you* feel that way, you're much less likely to stay with it and incorporate this important inner game exercise into your life. So allow me to clear up a couple of misconceptions before we continue.

First, there's really no "being bad" at Focused Sitting. Yes, it's true that your thoughts won't stay quiet for very long, especially at first (and sometimes they won't at all), but that doesn't mean you're not good at it or that you can't do it. The exercise is just giving you a clear look at the nature of your big, crazy brain. Our brains are thought-generating, distraction-making machines that, in my experience, never stop for more than a few seconds at a time. Expecting your thoughts to completely stop would be like going to the ocean and expecting the waves to stop. It's simply not in their nature.

Second, the exercise *can* feel like a struggle, but that's just the way it is. And it does get easier. Again, it has nothing to do with whether you're good at it. The truth is, it's still a struggle for me at times, and I've been doing it for over forty years. Sitting quietly sounds peaceful—and there certainly is a peaceful component "fight or flight" center); and decreased activation of the default-mode network, which contributes to stilling the random chatter of the mind. All of this helps you be more calm, lowers your stress, makes you more emotionally resilient, raises the quality of your thinking and creativity, and helps you be more present and focused. In other words, this exercise takes all the traits we're working to bring out through raising your inner game and *builds them into your system,* giving a massive boost to your efforts.

THE (NOT-SO) SECRET WEAPON OF ELITE PERFORMERS

As if all that weren't enough, here's one more reason to make this exercise a part of your daily life: Champions and elite-level performers in all walks of life are already doing it.

Focused Sitting is a form of meditation (specifically, of *Vipassana* meditation: a continued close attention to sensation, thoughts, and feelings), and meditation of one kind or another is a habit that a striking percentage of high-level performers have in common. Athletes, artists, entrepreneurs, soldiers, actors, CEOs, journalists, doctors, investment bankers, world leaders—the list goes on. And the reason they do it is because they know that a mental exercise like this is an indispensable part of operating at their highest level.

"I'M NOT VERY GOOD AT IT"

The first thing most people say after they try Focused Sitting is, "I'm not very good at it," by which they mean their thoughts aren't getting quiet and the exercise is a bit of a struggle, rather than being the peaceful experience they expected. The feelings are certainly understandable, but if *you* feel that way, you're much less likely to stay with it and incorporate this important inner game exercise into your life. So allow me to clear up a couple of misconceptions before we continue.

First, there's really no "being bad" at Focused Sitting. Yes, it's true that your thoughts won't stay quiet for very long, especially at first (and sometimes they won't at all), but that doesn't mean you're not good at it or that you can't do it. The exercise is just giving you a clear look at the nature of your big, crazy brain. Our brains are thought-generating, distraction-making machines that, in my experience, never stop for more than a few seconds at a time. Expecting your thoughts to completely stop would be like going to the ocean and expecting the waves to stop. It's simply not in their nature.

Second, the exercise *can* feel like a struggle, but that's just the way it is. And it does get easier. Again, it has nothing to do with whether you're good at it. The truth is, it's still a struggle for me at times, and I've been doing it for over forty years. Sitting quietly sounds peaceful—and there certainly is a peaceful component to it—but Focused Sitting is not inherently an exercise in peaceful bliss. It's an *exercise*, like any other.

Take running, for example. I don't always enjoy it. Sometimes I'm tired, sometimes my legs are heavy and I have to walk part of the way, sometimes the weather's nasty and the whole thing is an unpleasant slog. But even at those times, I know it's good for me, and I *always* feel good afterward. That's a much more realistic expectation of what it's like to do Focused Sitting: It's an exercise, plain and simple. It's a wonderful one that brings incredible benefits, but it's an exercise just the same—in raising your inner game.

So, as you start to incorporate Focused Sitting into your life, if you find yourself thinking you're not good at it and that maybe it's not for you, please just set that aside. There's no innate talent required. You simply sit, you drift, you pull yourself back. Some days it goes well; other days less so. The important thing is that you *do it*.

ONE PART OF A LARGER PROGRAM

With all I've said here about the benefits of Focused Sitting, you'd be forgiven for thinking that it's the *only* thing you need to do. But there's a reason this is the third tool we've discussed, rather than the first.

I didn't mention this in the introduction, but at the time of my Wizard-of-Oz moment, I had already been meditating for nearly twenty years. I was first introduced to Transcendental Meditation (TM) in 1973, when I was fourteen. And over the years, though I didn't do it every day by any means, I enjoyed many of the same benefits you hear so much about today (and that are listed above): reduced stress, increased creativity, increased focus and well-being, and so on. The point, though, is that by the time 1992 rolled around, even after my having meditated for some two decades, *my life was still slipping out of control.* Now, maybe I didn't do it often enough or I didn't do it correctly, or maybe I didn't go deep enough into the whole idea of mindfulness. All I know is that meditation alone wasn't enough for me, and I don't believe it's enough for you either.

The truth is, even with all the great things Focused Sitting does for you, meditation is sort of like going to a spa: It feels wonderful, and the glow stays with you, but it doesn't have the *practical impact* on your life that you want and need. Remember, what we're looking to do here is develop the three types of self-control we've been talking about—cognitive control, emotional self-regulation, and impulse control. Focused Sitting certainly helps with that, but for the kind of practical change we're looking for, it works best as part of a larger program—the kind of program presented in this book: You start with a clear understanding of how your inner game works, and then you work to incorporate *all four* skills and tools into your life.

Next up, the fourth tool.

CHAPTER 11

THE INNER GAME TRACKER

We've talked about three important skills and tools for rais-ing your inner game: Lifts, "No. Quiet," and Focused Sitting. And my hope is that you'll start using these right away and, ideally, turn them into habits as quickly as possible. Unfortunately, that's easier said than done. How many other good ideas have you heard (or had) over the years, that you sincerely meant to do, and perhaps even started doing, but didn't stay with?

Exactly.

All the knowledge and skills in the world won't make a difference unless you find a way to incorporate them into your life. That's where this last tool comes in. It's called the Inner Game Tracker, and its purpose is to help you stay engaged with raising your inner game in the weeks, months, and years to come.

A SIMPLE SPREADSHEET

The Inner Game Tracker is a spreadsheet in which you track various tasks and/or behaviors on a daily basis.

To get started, we'll track our three inner game tools, but the tracker works just as well with any behavior.

The first step is to create a new document in a spreadsheet application (e.g., Excel, Numbers, Google Sheets), with one column on the left for the date, one column for each behavior you want to track, and one column on the right for notes.

Here's how that would look in a typical spreadsheet:

Date	Lifts	"No. Quiet."	Focused Sitting	Note

Once you've got your sheet set up, you simply start using it. Each day, write in the date, indicate which items you did, and add any observations or other useful data in the "Note" column. Here's how your tracker might look after a couple of weeks:

Date	Lifts	"No. Quiet."	Focused Sitting	Note
Jan. 1	■	■	■	
1/2	■	■	■	
1/3	■	■		weekend
1/4	■	■	■	
1/5	■			
1/6	■	■	■	
1/7	■	■	■	
1/8	■	■	■	
1/9				got a cold?
1/10	■			
1/11	■	■	■	
1/12	■	■		
1/13	■			
1/14	■	■	■	
1/15				
1/16				
1/17				

Each row represents one day. Cells that are filled in are activities you did on that day. If you don't do an activity, that cell remains blank. So this serves as a record of your daily activities, and also gives you a quick visual of how engaged you were with your inner game over a given period of time.

**Don't Worry About Gaps in Your Sheet.
It's the Tracking That Matters.**

Looking at our example, you can see there are several gaps. Seeing that, you might think that this wasn't a good period; but it actually was, because you kept tracking the whole time, and tracking matters more than gaps. First of all, gaps happen. Some days, gravity gets the best of you. Other days, life just gets in the way. Small gaps like these are normal and nothing to be concerned about. The only time to worry is if you slip so far that you stop even *thinking* about doing the items on your sheet. But that generally won't happen until you've been away from tracking for a month or more. So, yes, the idea is to do the activities listed on your sheet as consistently as possible. They're good for you, it feels good to do them, and you feel better about yourself for having done them, which is why you put them on there in the first place. But if you miss a day, a few days, or even a week or two, don't worry too much. As long as you keep tracking, even if it's through some pretty big gaps, you're engaged with raising your inner game. And that, ultimately, is the most important thing.

As long as you keep tracking,
you're engaged with raising your inner game.

How Often You Do Each Behavior Is Up to You

The goal with the items we just put on your starter tracker is to do each one every day, because you want to make habits of the inner game tools as quickly as possible, and doing them every day for an initial period (typically thirty to sixty days) is the best way to achieve that. But for other behaviors, every day might not make sense. For example, exercising is another great thing to put on your tracker, but your preferred schedule for that might be every *other* day, or five days a week, or some other pattern that works for you.

Ultimately, every item you put on your tracking sheet should:

- Improve your life
- Make you feel proud of yourself for doing it
- Be something you can realistically do several times a week

Beyond that, how often you do it is up to you.

You Can Change Your Tracker Whenever You Want

Putting something on your Inner Game Tracker doesn't mean you're committing to doing it forever. You work on each item for as long as you want. As new ideas come up for behaviors you'd like to work on, just add a column for them and start tracking. When something becomes a habit, or you're no longer interested in tracking it for whatever reason, you can simply delete that column. In other words, it's easy to adjust your Inner Game Tracker so that it supports your changing interests and needs.

THE POWER IN TRACKING NEGATIVE BEHAVIORS

The purpose of the Inner Game Tracker, as I've said, is to help you stay engaged with raising your inner game in the weeks, months, and years to come—and it's the perfect tool for that. It's also very helpful for adding positive behaviors to your life. But its greatest impact on your inner game comes when you use it to also track negative behaviors.

A friend admitted to me that he has a terrible weakness for licorice. If he opens a bag of licorice, he'll keep eating until it's gone. He can't stop himself. That's what I mean by a *negative behavior*. It's a bad habit that doesn't officially rise to the level of being a serious addiction, but exhibits the same basic dynamic—you feel an ongoing compulsion for something that you can't completely control.

A person can develop a "bad" habit around almost anything. (Mine? Online news, checking my phone, Coke, and fatty/sugary foods.) But there's a special relationship between bad habits and your inner game that makes tracking and ultimately controlling them one of the most powerful things you can do.

Bad Habits: The Make-or-Break Factor

I discovered this by accident after I'd been using my Inner Game Tracker for a while. (My tracker has eight to ten items, split roughly evenly between the positive behaviors I want to add to my life and the bad habits I want to avoid.) Here's what I noticed: Whenever I gave in to a bad habit, I was weak with everything else on my sheet. It was a nearly perfect correlation. And it continues to this day. If I slip with one item in the morning—say, checking the news—it's much more likely I'll slip with others throughout the day, both positive and negative. I'll have a Coke. And another. I'll check my phone constantly and eat sweets. I won't go for a run. I won't do Focused Sitting. It's like kryptonite for Superman: Giving in to a compulsion saps all my strength for resisting gravity. And it also works the other way around: When I'm *avoiding* my bad habits, I'm *stronger* with everything else. And I feel great: focused, present, awake, energized—everything I want to be.

The lesson here, and it's an important one, is that *controlling your compulsive behaviors is the make-or-break factor of raising your inner game.* If you can't do this, the rest of the work is going to be much more difficult, if not impossible.

The Explanation: Awake Versus Sleepwalking

Raising your inner game is fundamentally about being awake rather than sleepwalking through your life.

Awake is when *you* are in control; sleepwalking is when the *levels* are in control. Giving in to a compulsion is sleepwalking because the unconscious impulses from your lower levels are dictating your behavior—and the more powerful the compulsion, the deeper your sleep becomes. That's why slipping with one or two bad habits can create such a drag on everything else. You're not simply slipping with those items; you're *putting yourself to sleep,* which ripples out into every area of your life.

> Slipping with one or two bad habits can create a drag on everything else, because you're not simply slipping with those items; you're *putting yourself to sleep,* which ripples out into every area of your life.

It's also why controlling bad habits makes such a profoundly positive difference. Not only do you get the direct benefit of avoiding the particular behavior, it also helps you be more awake and present in every area of your life.

Having said that, please don't stress out about every slip with your bad habits. It's still true that tracking is more important than gaps. The main thing here is to understand the critical role compulsive behavior plays in the larger mission of raising your inner game—and, of course, to get control of those bad habits.

The Inner Game Tracker is just one of the four inner game skills and tools, but it's the one that brings all the others together. Essentially, it's the hub—and gauge—of your inner work. When you're using your tracker, you're working on your inner game. When you're not, you're slipping. It really is as simple as that. So you want to get started using this right away. It only takes a few minutes to set up (and even less to use), but it's an incredibly helpful and powerful tool. And remember: Perfect is not the goal. *Engaged* is the goal. My tracker goes back years, and there are more empty cells than ones filled in. But I'm in the game, and that's the important thing.

If you're in, you win.

CHAPTER 12

ACTION STEPS

The goal of this book is to help you get stronger, mentally and emotionally, so that you can do your best work and, as it says on the cover, "live a life you're proud of every day."

Using the skills and tools we've covered in Part Two is how you do that.

When you're upset or worried about something, and you can't stop thinking about it, "No. Quiet" helps you control your thoughts and stay focused. When you're feeling stressed and acting negative and testy, not being the person you want to be, Lifts help you snap out of it and stay present and positive. When your attempts at thinking through a problem haven't yielded a solution, Focused Sitting and "No. Quiet" help you go deeper and find the answers you need. When fear is holding you back, or when emotions rise up and threaten to make you say or do something you'll regret, resisting and saying "Nope, not going there. Quiet," keeps it from happening. When bad habits are getting the best of you, the Inner Game Tracker and Focused Sitting help build your willpower and put *you* back in control. This is what raising your inner game looks like, and the resulting transformation shows up in every area of our lives—from practical examples like these all the way to the deepest questions we have about who we are and our place in the world.

Now it's time to put all this into action. Here's what you should do right now, today, and over the next week to get started. Some of this may seem self-evident, but I want to be crystal clear as to the specific tasks to be done. Now, the truth is, it's not absolutely necessary to do all of the items on this list. You could simply start using the skills and tools and be on your way. But this is what I recommend in order to maximize your efforts and chances for success:

1. Reread the book. As my good friend and *QBQ!* co-author John G. Miller likes to say, "Repetition is the motor of learning." Once you've finished reading these last few chapters, the best thing you can do to anchor the material and accelerate your early progress is to read through the book again before you begin the actual work.

2. Set up your tracking sheet. Your Inner Game Tracker is what keeps you engaged with raising your inner game, so you want to get in the habit of using this as quickly as possible. If you haven't done it already, once you've finished rereading the book, set up your tracker right away.

3. Create reminders for each item you're tracking, and put them where you'll see them. The hard part of keeping a tracking sheet isn't the items themselves, which typically aren't difficult or time consuming. The hard part is *remembering to do them*. Even with our best intentions, gravity has a way of making us forget and go back to the way things were. Fortunately, there's an easy solution. It's simply a matter of posting reminders where they'll demand your attention. Some people put sticky notes on their computer monitor. Personally, I use my Mac Calendar and a to-do list app (OmniFocus). There are many ways this can be done. The keys, again, are to create one reminder for each item you're tracking and to put them where you're guaranteed to see them.

4. *Go!* Once you've completed steps 1-3, you're ready to go. Start using the skills, avoiding your bad habits, and tracking your activities.

5. Start an Inner Game Journal. Keeping a journal is the secret ingredient for success with any project, especially one that involves inner work. It helps you think things through and find answers to the questions and challenges that come up. It gives you perspective and clarity, evening out the ups and downs, and helps mark your progress, reminding you of how far you've come. Whether you use pen and paper, a word processing program on your computer, or an app such as Evernote or Five Minute Journal, an Inner Game Journal is a very helpful tool. Make your first entry as soon as you've begun your daily tracking, and then plan to keep with it as a regular part of raising your inner game.

6. Explore the additional resources at davidlevin.com/ryig. On the *Raise Your Inner Game* page on my website, I've put together a collection of inner game resources that I've found helpful over the years. Quotes, stories, book recommendations, blog posts, songs, links to other resources—it's all there, along with free training and special offers. It's true that we've already covered everything you need in order to raise your inner game, and to continue raising it in the weeks, months, and years to come. But that doesn't mean there aren't other things that you'll find helpful along the way, and every little bit makes it that much easier to stay on track and be successful.

Once you have everything else set up and running, take some time to check out these additional resources as well. I'm sure you'll find them as helpful as I have.

Finally, when you're ready to go, I recommend starting with a thirty-day challenge. Commit yourself to following your plan to the letter for the next thirty days—no slips, no excuses, whatever it takes. This will help you feel the benefits right away, push through any initial resistance, and accelerate your momentum.

CHAPTER 13

THE ROAD AHEAD

You now have everything you need to raise your inner game: You know how the inner game works, you have the skills and tools to do it, and you have a step-by-step plan for getting started. Assuming you're going forward, here's what you can expect on the road ahead.

Phase One: A New Baseline

At first, as with anything, this will all be new and interesting. You'll start using the skills and tools, and feeling the difference they make. You'll also find that, once you get started, you'll naturally want to continue, because it feels so much better to be more awake and to operate at a higher level. So, very quickly, you'll develop a new, higher standard for what your everyday life should feel like. You'll also become more aware of what it feels like when you're *not* in this state. So this higher level becomes your new baseline, and you get pretty attached to it, because, again, it feels so much more alive and satisfying.

Phase Two: Find the Balance Point

Once you have your new baseline established, the next phase is discovering what it takes to stay there.

During the initial period, as I said, you get very familiar with, and attached to, what it feels like to be on this new, higher level. And, of course, using the skills and tools is what gets you there. But then you start to bump into the realities of your life: You get distracted, you get sick, you lose your focus, and so on. So maybe you don't do Focused Sitting for a week or two, or you stop thinking about Lifts, or some of your bad habits start to creep back in. As I said in Chapter Eleven, this is all normal and nothing to be too concerned about. But at some point, as a result, you'll notice that you're not being your new self anymore—you're slipping back into your old ways, getting stressed and distracted again, and not feeling as strong and positive as you were. So then (because this is not the person you want to be anymore), you'll pick back up with doing the items on your tracking sheet. But this time, instead of shooting for doing Focused Sitting every day, maybe you'll try four or five days a week, and instead of completely avoiding soda (which doesn't seem to be working), you'll try limiting it to once a week.

That's what happens during Phase Two: You slip, you pull yourself back, you experiment, you figure out what works for you until, finally, you find the balance point, where you're clear as to where you want to be, and you know just how much inner game work it takes to keep yourself at that level.

Phase Three: Inner Game Mastery
Once you have your new baseline established and you know what it takes to sustain it, from then on *you're in control of your inner game:* You can keep yourself where you want to be no matter what changes come up in your life—you simply adjust the intensity of your inner game work to fit the new situation.

Here's an example of this from recent experience.

The 2016 U.S. presidential election was a high-gravity period for me. I've mentioned earlier that online news is one of my bad habits, and it's actually the one that I most need to avoid if I want to stay strong with the rest of my inner game. But during this period, the pull I felt to follow along with the election was overpowering. For four months I fell off the wagon, so to speak, with checking the news. There were three different websites that I would visit at least ten times a day, giving me a constant barrage of lower-level triggers—fear, anxiety, confusion, anger—and I could really feel the effect of all this on my inner state. But during that same time, I was also writing this book, which meant I needed to be able to focus and think at my highest level, not to mention wanting to continue to be present and positive with my family and friends. So, to compensate for the increase in gravity, I got much more disciplined with the skills and tools, and with my tracking sheet items: I was more consistent with Focused Sitting and getting exercise and doing Lifts, and was more strict about avoiding the rest of my bad habits. And it worked. In spite of the increase in stress and distraction, I was able to work at the level I needed and to remain the person I wanted to be. And when the election was over, I just dialed my efforts back to their normal level and continued on.

That's what Inner Game Mastery looks like. It doesn't mean you won't have rough periods. It doesn't make you any sort of special person. It simply means you can get yourself to whatever level you need and continue to be the person you want to be, no matter what else is happening in your life—or what's happening in the world.

WHY THIS MATTERS NOW

I'm not a mental health professional, but looking around the world today, it seems to me that people everywhere are going a little crazy. Defensive, angry, belligerent, fearful—it's pretty remarkable. Now, when you look at how incredibly stressful and fast-paced our lives have become, and you know that stress and pressure trigger lower-level behavior, the situation is not that hard to understand. Nevertheless, the stress and pressure are not going away anytime soon. In fact, they'll almost certainly continue to increase, which means that the negative behaviors we're seeing are likely to *also* get worse—unless people learn the new skills we've been talking about.

The bottom line here is that the process we just discussed helps you master your inner game, and the more people there are in the world who can do that, the better off we're all going to be.

"MORE ALIVE"

The last thing to say about what to expect going forward is that much of what we've talked about throughout this book can give the impression that raising your inner game will make your life quieter and more peaceful. But what it really does is make you feel more *alive,* which is not the same thing at all.

When you're more awake and present in your life, you notice things that you didn't notice before. You're more aware of what's happening around you and inside of you, and are more tuned in to subtle differences in your inner state and to the effect things have on you. With all this new input and things to pay attention to, your higher baseline can actually feel noisier, in a sense, and require more energy on your part. But it also feels more joyful and connected, and is much more satisfying and fulfilling. So the best expectation for the road ahead is not that it will be more peaceful and serene, but that it will just be *more.* More vibrant. More colorful. More energized. More beautiful. More like life is meant to be.

CONCLUSION

RAISE YOUR INNER GAME!

The sole meaning of life is to serve humanity.
—Leo Tolstoy

I've said a lot throughout this book about the difference that raising your inner game makes in your life, and it truly is remarkable (and exciting, because you're about to discover that difference for yourself). But as we finish up, I also want you to understand the impact your work can have on others, because this may be the best reason of all to raise your inner game.

In Chapter Five, in the section on *high-gravity triggers*, I said, "People can be the biggest high-gravity triggers of all," meaning that when someone's in a strong lower-level state, it pulls down everyone around them (and I'm sure you've seen this yourself, where one person's negativity pulls down an entire group). But the good news is that this same dynamic also works in the opposite direction. That is, when someone's at their *best* (operating from Level 4), it lifts others *up*.

Unfortunately, getting pulled down is much more common than being lifted up. For some reason, negativity comes more naturally to people—and spreads more easily. But that's exactly why it's so helpful to be able to break this cycle and resist our inner gravity.

So these are the gifts you give to others when you raise your inner game: First, you lift them up and inspire them to be their best. Co-workers, customers, friends, family—every one of them feels the difference. This alone is reason enough to do it, in my opinion (and, I expect, in Tolstoy's). There's no higher purpose than to serve the people in our lives, and we do that by being the best person we can possibly be.

The second gift is that you're helping to counter the problem we talked about in the previous chapter—the stress and negativity that are affecting so many people around the world today. It might not seem like you could make much difference with this, given that you're just one person, but one-person-at-a-time is the only way it can be done—resisting gravity, raising your inner game, and setting an example for others to do the same.

The first gift, helping others, gives you a more direct benefit (it's deeply satisfying to make a positive difference in people's lives); but I actually find this second one to be the most inspiring, because this is where the work feels like it's "making a dent in the universe," as Steve Jobs famously put it.

In any case, whichever reason is the most inspiring to you, I truly believe that raising your inner game is the most important work any of us can do. And you now have everything you need to do it.

At this point, the only thing standing in your way is me continuing on. So let me finish with this: Steve Prefontaine, the legendary long-distance runner, said, "To give anything less than your best is to sacrifice your gift."

Don't sacrifice your gift.

You have a chance to do something important here—for yourself, for the people in your life, and for the world.

Give us your best.

Raise your inner game!

Acknowledgments

First, I want to thank my editor, Kelle Walsh. I shudder to think what this book would have been like without her. Between her skills as an editor and her deep understanding of the inner world, she was the perfect person to help bring *RYIG* to life. Kelle, I can't thank you enough. Also, to Ryan Holiday at Brass Checks for his invaluable feedback. Painful to hear, but what a difference. More shudders, and huge thanks.

I'm grateful also to the production team: Jon Valk, for again coming up with the perfect cover (that's three in a row!); Karen Minster, for making the printed book into the art I hoped it would be; Joni McPherson, for the great illustrations; and Richard Bock, for the author picture. Thanks, everyone, for your excellent work.

Next, it's a cliché to thank one's parents, but in this case, there's actually a link because they're the ones who put me on the inner game path in the first place. My father, among his many inspirations, is the person who drove me, flowers and fruit in hand, across the bay to Berkeley, California, to learn Transcendental

Meditation. And Mom, of course, has always been the prime believer. I love you both very much.

Thanks again to the key influencers I mentioned: Timothy Gallwey, for *The Inner Game of Tennis* (and for coining the term "inner game" in the first place); Eckhart Tolle, whose books *The Power of Now* and *A New Earth* helped me finally understand the meaning of *presence*; and Sam Harris, whose *The End of Faith* inspired me to discover the power of seeing the inner game in a secular light. I also want to mention Josh Waitzkin, whose *The Art of Learning* helped me see more clearly the relationship between stillness and peak creativity. I didn't do his ideas justice, but they helped me improve the creativity segments immensely.

Special thanks to the early readers for their helpful (and encouraging) comments: Les McPherson, Lisa LaBrie, Carla Camins Macapinlac, Lacey Filipich, Sharon Martin, Kenneth J. Coleman, Georgine Madden, Brad Kynoch, Rob Ashton, and Larry Preston.

And finally, to my family—Margret, Peter, Frances, and Aaron. "Love" doesn't begin to express what I feel for you. You're simply everything to me. My greatest hope is that I've managed my inner game well enough so that you know how true that is, now and forever.

About the Author

In 1992, David Levin was a struggling singer-songwriter whose career (and life) were going nowhere. But then he had a strange, Wizard of Oz moment that totally changed the arc of his life. Four albums, five books, and twenty-nine years of happy marriage later, he's condensed what he's learned into a simple, practical guide for how to be stronger, mentally and emotionally, so that you can do your best work and live a life you're proud of every day.

David is the co-author (with John G. Miller) of the million-selling book *QBQ! The Question Behind the Question*, the author of *Don't Just Talk, Be Heard!* and the creator of the Focused! Every Day training program. He is also an award-winning songwriter and recording artist, and lives happily ever after in Viroqua, Wisconsin, with his wife and children.

Visit David and discover
additional inner game resources at
www.davidlevin.com.